SOUND™
INNOVATIONS

ENSEMBLE DEVELOPMENT

Chorales and Warm-up Exercises for Tone, Technique and Rhythm

ADVANCED CONCERT BAND

Peter **BOONSHAFT** | Chris **BERNOTAS**

Thank you for making *Sound Innovations: Ensemble Development for Advanced Concert Band* a part of your concert band curriculum. With 399 exercises, including over 70 chorales by some of today's most renowned composers for concert band, it is our hope you will find this book to be a valuable resource in helping you grow in your understanding and abilities as an ensemble musician.

An assortment of exercises are grouped by key and presented in a variety of difficulty levels. Where possible, several exercises in the same category are provided to allow for variety while accomplishing the goals of that specific type of exercise. You will notice that many exercises and chorales are clearly marked with dynamics, articulations, style, and tempo for you to practice those aspects of performance. Other exercises are intentionally left for you or your teacher to determine how best to use them in reaching your performance goals.

Whether you are progressing through exercises to better your technical facility or to challenge your musicianship with beautiful chorales, we are confident you will be excited, motivated, and inspired by using *Sound Innovations: Ensemble Development for Advanced Concert Band*.

D1538143

Alfred

© 2014 Alfred Music
Sound Innovations™ is a trademark of Alfred Music
All Rights Reserved including Public Performance

ISBN-10: 1-4706-1815-X
ISBN-13: 978-1-4706-1815-5

Instrument photos courtesy of Yamaha Corporation of America Band & Orchestral Division

Concert B♭ Major (Your C Major)

1 **PASSING THE TONIC**

2 **PASSING THE TONIC**

3 **PASSING THE TONIC**

4 **LONG TONES**

5 **LONG TONES**

6 **LONG TONES**

7 **CONCERT B♭ MAJOR SCALE**

8 **SCALE PATTERN**

16 ARPEGGIOS

17 ARPEGGIOS

18 INTERVALS

19 INTERVALS

20 BALANCE AND INTONATION: PERFECT INTERVALS

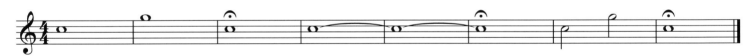

21 BALANCE AND INTONATION: DIATONIC HARMONY

22 BALANCE AND INTONATION: LAYERED TUNING

23 BALANCE AND INTONATION: MOVING CHORD TONES

24 BALANCE AND INTONATION: SHIFTING CHORD QUALITIES

25 EXPANDING INTERVALS: DOWNWARD IN PARALLEL OCTAVES

26 EXPANDING INTERVALS: UPWARD IN PARALLEL FIFTHS

27 EXPANDING INTERVALS: DOWNWARD IN TRIADS

28 EXPANDING INTERVALS: UPWARD IN TRIADS

29 RHYTHM: SIMPLE METER ($\frac{4}{4}$)

30 RHYTHM: COMPOUND METER ($\frac{6}{8}$)

31 RHYTHMIC SUBDIVISION

32 CHANGING METER $\frac{6}{8}$ AND $\frac{3}{4}$

33 CHANGING METER $\frac{4}{4}$ AND $\frac{5}{8}$

34 CONCERT B♭ MAJOR SCALE AND CHORALE — Chris M. Bernotas (ASCAP)

35 CHORALE — Randall D. Standridge (ASCAP)

36 CHORALE — Rossano Galante

37 CHORALE — Jack Stamp

38 CHORALE — David R. Gillingham

39 CHORALE — Andrew Boysen, Jr.

Concert G Minor (Your A Minor)

47 PASSING THE TONIC

48 LONG TONES

49 CONCERT G NATURAL MINOR SCALE

50 CONCERT G HARMONIC AND MELODIC MINOR SCALES

51 SCALE PATTERN

52 SCALE PATTERN

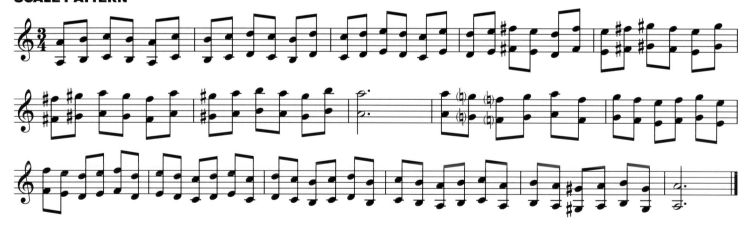

53 FLEXIBILITY

54 CHROMATIC FLEXIBILITY

55 ARPEGGIOS

56 ARPEGGIOS

57 INTERVALS

58 INTERVALS

59 BALANCE AND INTONATION: DIATONIC HARMONY

60 BALANCE AND INTONATION: MOVING CHORD TONES

61 BALANCE AND INTONATION: LAYERED TUNING

62 BALANCE AND INTONATION: FAMILY BALANCE

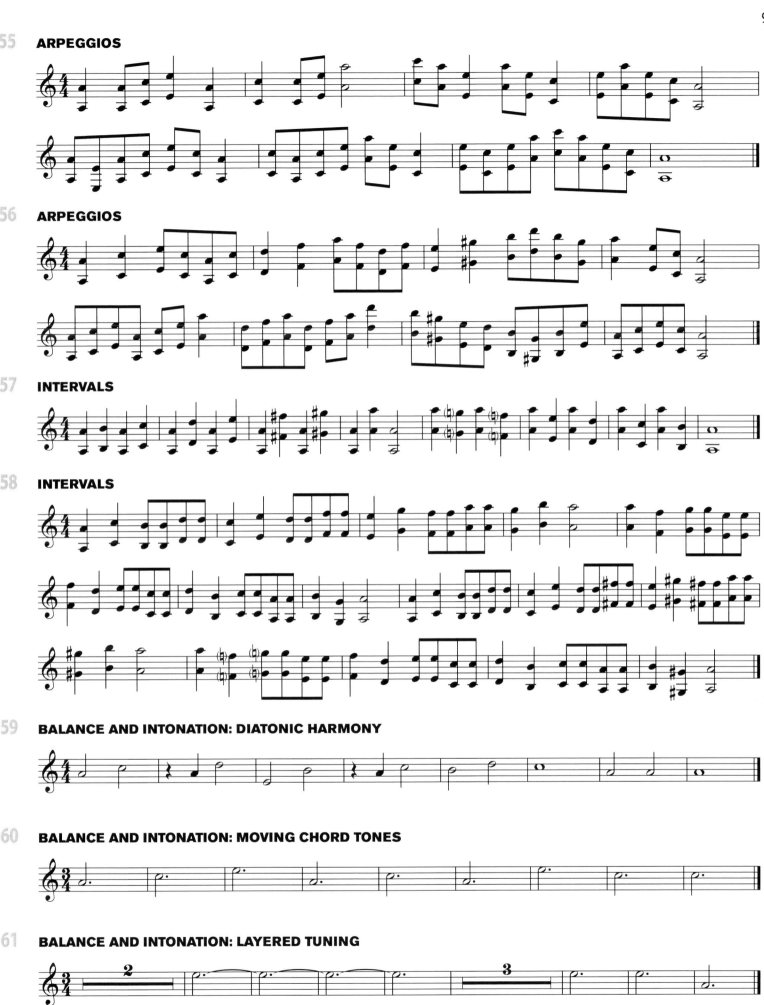

63 EXPANDING INTERVALS: DOWNWARD IN PARALLEL OCTAVES

64 EXPANDING INTERVALS: DOWNWARD IN TRIADS

65 EXPANDING INTERVALS: UPWARD IN TRIADS

66 RHYTHM: SIMPLE METER ($\frac{4}{4}$)

67 RHYTHM: COMPOUND METER ($\frac{3}{8}$)

68 RHYTHMIC SUBDIVISION

69 CHANGING METER $\frac{3}{4}$ AND $\frac{6}{8}$

Concert E♭ Major (Your F Major)

76 **PASSING THE TONIC**

77 **PASSING THE TONIC**

78 **PASSING THE TONIC**

79 **LONG TONES**

80 **LONG TONES**

81 **LONG TONES**

82 **CONCERT E♭ MAJOR SCALE**

83 **SCALE PATTERN**

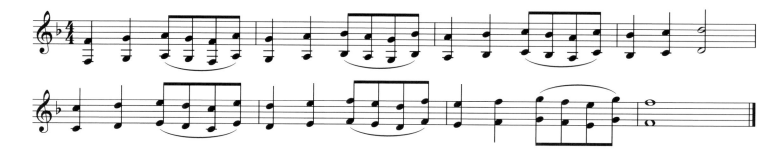

84 SCALE PATTERN

85 CONCERT E♭ CHROMATIC SCALE

86 CHROMATIC SCALE PATTERN

87 FLEXIBILITY

88 FLEXIBILITY

89 FLEXIBILITY

90 CHROMATIC FLEXIBILITY

91 **ARPEGGIOS**

92 **ARPEGGIOS**

93 **INTERVALS**

94 **INTERVALS**

95 **BALANCE AND INTONATION: PERFECT INTERVALS**

96 **BALANCE AND INTONATION: DIATONIC HARMONY**

97 **BALANCE AND INTONATION: LAYERED TUNING**

98 **BALANCE AND INTONATION: MOVING CHORD TONES**

99 **BALANCE AND INTONATION: SHIFTING CHORD QUALITIES**

100 EXPANDING INTERVALS: DOWNWARD IN PARALLEL OCTAVES

101 EXPANDING INTERVALS: DOWNWARD IN PARALLEL FIFTHS

102 EXPANDING INTERVALS: DOWNWARD IN TRIADS

103 EXPANDING INTERVALS: UPWARD IN TRIADS

104 RHYTHM: SIMPLE METER (4/4)

105 RHYTHM: COMPOUND METER (12/8)

106 RHYTHMIC SUBDIVISION

107 CHANGING METER 4/4 AND 3/8

108 CHANGING METER 3/4 AND 5/8

109 **CONCERT E♭ MAJOR SCALE AND CHORALE**

Chris M. Bernotas (ASCAP)

110 **CHORALE**

Ralph Ford (ASCAP)

Gentle

111 **CHORALE**

Roland Barrett (ASCAP)

Gracefully

112 **CHORALE**

Randall D. Standridge

113 **CHORALE**

Rossano Galante

Andante

114 **CHORALE**

Chris M. Bernotas (ASCAP)

Sweetly

Concert C Minor (Your D Minor)

121 **PASSING THE TONIC**

122 **LONG TONES**

123 **CONCERT C NATURAL MINOR SCALE**

124 **CONCERT C HARMONIC AND MELODIC MINOR SCALES**

125 **SCALE PATTERN**

126 **SCALE PATTERN**

127 **FLEXIBILITY**

128 **CHROMATIC FLEXIBILITY**

129 ARPEGGIOS

130 ARPEGGIOS

131 INTERVALS

132 INTERVALS

133 BALANCE AND INTONATION: DIATONIC HARMONY

134 BALANCE AND INTONATION: MOVING CHORD TONES

135 BALANCE AND INTONATION: LAYERED TUNING

136 BALANCE AND INTONATION: FAMILY BALANCE

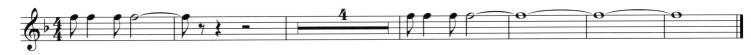

137 EXPANDING INTERVALS: DOWNWARD IN PARALLEL OCTAVES

138 EXPANDING INTERVALS: DOWNWARD IN TRIADS

139 EXPANDING INTERVALS: UPWARD IN TRIADS

140 RHYTHM ($\frac{5}{4}$)

141 RHYTHM: COMPOUND METER ($\frac{6}{8}$)

142 RHYTHMIC SUBDIVISION

143 CHANGING METER: $\frac{4}{4}$ AND $\frac{7}{8}$

Concert F Major (Your G Major)

150 **PASSING THE TONIC**

151 **LONG TONES**

152 **CONCERT F MAJOR SCALE**

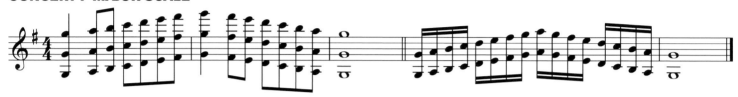

153 **CONCERT F CHROMATIC SCALE**

154 **SCALE PATTERN**

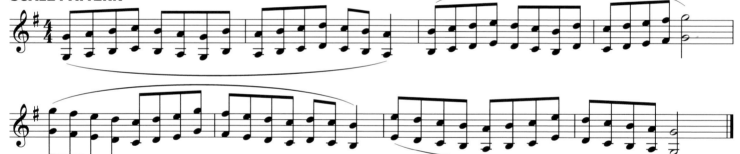

155 **SCALE PATTERN**

156 **FLEXIBILITY**

157 **CHROMATIC FLEXIBILITY**

158 **ARPEGGIOS**

159 **ARPEGGIOS**

160 **INTERVALS**

161 **INTERVALS**

162 **BALANCE AND INTONATION: DIATONIC HARMONY**

163 **BALANCE AND INTONATION: MOVING CHORD TONES**

164 **BALANCE AND INTONATION: LAYERED TUNING**

165 **BALANCE AND INTONATION: FAMILY BALANCE**

166 **EXPANDING INTERVALS: DOWNWARD IN PARALLEL OCTAVES**

167 **EXPANDING INTERVALS: DOWNWARD IN TRIADS**

168 **EXPANDING INTERVALS: UPWARD IN TRIADS**

169 **RHYTHM: SIMPLE METER (4/4)**

170 **RHYTHM: COMPOUND METER (9/8)**

171 **RHYTHMIC SUBDIVISION**

172 **CHANGING METER: 4/4 AND 7/8**

173 **CONCERT F MAJOR SCALE AND CHORALE**

Chris M. Bernotas (ASCAP)

174 **CHORALE**

Roland Barrett (ASCAP)

175 **CHORALE**

Rossano Galante

176 **CHORALE**

Chris M. Bernotas (ASCAP)

177 **CHORALE**

David R. Gillingham

178 **CHORALE**

Jack Stamp

Concert D Minor (Your E Minor)

179 PASSING THE TONIC

180 LONG TONES

181 CONCERT D NATURAL MINOR SCALE

182 CONCERT D HARMONIC AND MELODIC MINOR SCALES

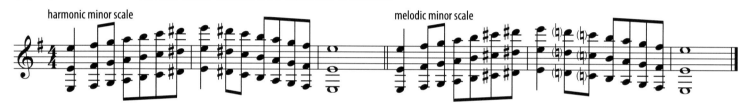

183 SCALE PATTERN

184 SCALE PATTERN

185 FLEXIBILITY

186 CHROMATIC FLEXIBILITY

187 ARPEGGIOS

188 ARPEGGIOS

189 INTERVALS

190 INTERVALS

191 BALANCE AND INTONATION: DIATONIC HARMONY

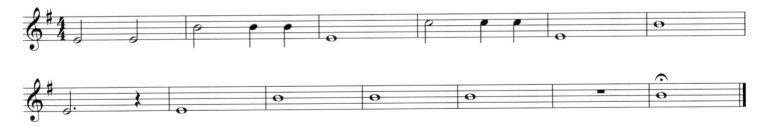

192 BALANCE AND INTONATION: MOVING CHORD TONES

193 BALANCE AND INTONATION: LAYERED TUNING

194 BALANCE AND INTONATION: FAMILY BALANCE

195 EXPANDING INTERVALS: DOWNWARD IN PARALLEL OCTAVES

196 EXPANDING INTERVALS: DOWNWARD IN TRIADS

197 EXPANDING INTERVALS: UPWARD IN TRIADS

198 RHYTHM (6/4)

199 RHYTHM: COMPOUND METER (6/8)

200 RHYTHMIC SUBDIVISION

201 CHANGING METER: 4/4 AND 7/8

(2+3+2)

202 CONCERT D MINOR SCALE AND CHORALE — Chris M. Bernotas (ASCAP)

203 CHORALE — Robert Sheldon
Somber

204 CHORALE — Michael Story (ASCAP)
Andante

205 CHORALE — Chris M. Bernotas (ASCAP)
Andante

206 CHORALE: PRÄLUDIUM — Arcangelo Corelli (1653–1713), Edited and Arranged by Todd Stalter
Adagio

207 CHORALE — Rossano Galante
Lento

Concert A♭ Major (Your B♭ Major)

208 PASSING THE TONIC

209 LONG TONES

210 CONCERT A♭ MAJOR SCALE

211 SCALE PATTERN

212 SCALE PATTERN

213 CONCERT A♭ CHROMATIC SCALE

214 FLEXIBILITY

215 CHROMATIC FLEXIBILITY

216 **ARPEGGIOS**

217 **ARPEGGIOS**

218 **INTERVALS**

219 **INTERVALS**

220 **BALANCE AND INTONATION: DIATONIC HARMONY**

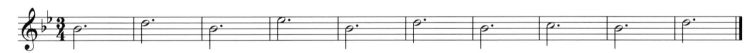

221 **BALANCE AND INTONATION: MOVING CHORD TONES**

222 **BALANCE AND INTONATION: LAYERED TUNING**

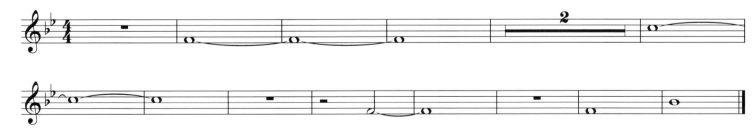

223 **BALANCE AND INTONATION: FAMILY BALANCE**

224 **EXPANDING INTERVALS: DOWNWARD IN PARALLEL OCTAVES**

225 **EXPANDING INTERVALS: DOWNWARD IN TRIADS**

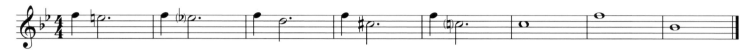

226 **EXPANDING INTERVALS: UPWARD IN TRIADS**

227 **RHYTHM: SIMPLE METER (4/4)**

228 **RHYTHM: COMPOUND METER (9/8)**

229 **RHYTHMIC SUBDIVISION (4/4)**

230 **CHANGING METER: 4/4 AND 6/8 AND 3/4**

Concert F Minor (Your G Minor)

237 PASSING THE TONIC

238 LONG TONES

239 CONCERT F NATURAL MINOR SCALE

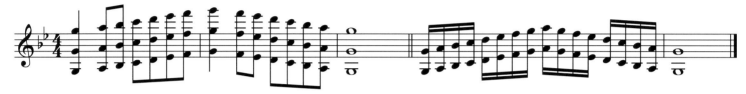

240 CONCERT F HARMONIC AND MELODIC MINOR SCALES

241 SCALE PATTERN

242 SCALE PATTERN

243 FLEXIBILITY

244 CHROMATIC FLEXIBILITY

245 ARPEGGIOS

246 ARPEGGIOS

247 INTERVALS

248 INTERVALS

249 BALANCE AND INTONATION: DIATONIC HARMONY

250 BALANCE AND INTONATION: MOVING CHORD TONES

251 BALANCE AND INTONATION: LAYERED TUNING

252 BALANCE AND INTONATION: FAMILY BALANCE

253 **EXPANDING INTERVALS: DOWNWARD IN PARALLEL OCTAVES**

254 **EXPANDING INTERVALS: DOWNWARD IN TRIADS**

255 **EXPANDING INTERVALS: UPWARD IN TRIADS**

256 **RHYTHM: SIMPLE METER (3/4)**

257 **RHYTHM: COMPOUND METER (12/8)**

258 **RHYTHMIC SUBDIVISION**

259 **CHANGING METER: 4/4 AND 5/8**

38

Concert D♭/C♯ Major (Your E♭ Major)

266 PASSING THE TONIC

267 LONG TONES

268 CONCERT D♭/C♯ MAJOR SCALE

269 SCALE PATTERN

270 SCALE PATTERN

271 FLEXIBILITY

272 CHROMATIC FLEXIBILITY

273 ARPEGGIOS

274 INTERVALS

275 BALANCE AND INTONATION: MOVING CHORD TONES

276 BALANCE AND INTONATION: SHIFTING CHORD QUALITIES

277 EXPANDING INTERVALS: DOWNWARD IN PARALLEL OCTAVES

278 EXPANDING INTERVALS: UPWARD IN PARALLEL FIFTHS

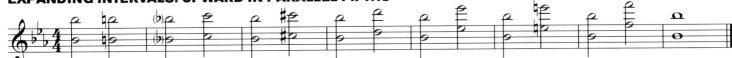

279 CONCERT D♭ MAJOR SCALE AND CHORALE

Chris M. Bernotas (ASCAP)

280 CHORALE

Chris M. Bernotas (ASCAP)

281 CHORALE

Roland Barrett (ASCAP)

Concert B♭ Minor (Your C Minor)

282 **PASSING THE TONIC**

283 **CONCERT B♭ NATURAL MINOR SCALE**

284 **CONCERT B♭ HARMONIC AND MELODIC MINOR SCALES**

harmonic minor scale

melodic minor scale

285 **SCALE PATTERN**

286 **SCALE PATTERN**

287 **FLEXIBILITY**

288 **ARPEGGIOS**

289 **INTERVALS**

290 **BALANCE AND INTONATION: LAYERED TUNING**

291 **BALANCE AND INTONATION: DIATONIC HARMONY**

292 **EXPANDING INTERVALS: DOWNWARD IN TRIADS**

293 **EXPANDING INTERVALS: UPWARD IN TRIADS**

294 **CONCERT Bb MINOR SCALE AND CHORALE**

Chris M. Bernotas (ASCAP)

295 **CHORALE**

Stephen Melillo (ASCAP)

296 **CHORALE**

Ralph Ford (ASCAP)

Concert C Major (Your D Major)

297 **PASSING THE TONIC**

298 **CONCERT C MAJOR SCALE**

299 **SCALE PATTERN**

300 **SCALE PATTERN**

301 **FLEXIBILITY**

302 **ARPEGGIOS**

303 **INTERVALS**

304 BALANCE AND INTONATION: MOVING CHORD TONES

305 BALANCE AND INTONATION: LAYERED TUNING

306 EXPANDING INTERVALS: DOWNWARD IN PARALLEL OCTAVES

307 EXPANDING INTERVALS: UPWARD IN PARALLEL FIFTHS

308 CONCERT C MAJOR SCALE AND CHORALE

Chris M. Bernotas (ASCAP)

A

B

309 CHORALE

Chris M. Bernotas (ASCAP)

Flowing

mf *f*

11

2

3

p

mf < *f* *p*

310 CHORALE

Robert Sheldon

Gently

mf *f*

9 A tempo

mp *rall.* *mf* *rall.*

Concert A Minor (Your B Minor)

311 PASSING THE TONIC

312 CONCERT A NATURAL MINOR SCALE

313 CONCERT A HARMONIC AND MELODIC MINOR SCALES

314 SCALE PATTERN

315 SCALE PATTERN

316 FLEXIBILITY

317 ARPEGGIOS

318 INTERVALS

319 BALANCE AND INTONATION: MOVING CHORD TONES

45

320 BALANCE AND INTONATION: DIATONIC HARMONY

321 EXPANDING INTERVALS: DOWNWARD IN PARALLEL OCTAVES

322 EXPANDING INTERVALS: DOWNWARD IN TRIADS

323 CONCERT A MINOR SCALE AND CHORALE

Chris M. Bernotas (ASCAP)

324 CHORALE

Randall D. Standridge

325 CHORALE: AIR, HWV 467

Georg Fredrich Handel (1685–1759)
Edited and Arranged by Todd Stalter

Concert G Major (Your A Major)

326 **PASSING THE TONIC**

327 **CONCERT G MAJOR SCALE**

328 **SCALE PATTERN**

329 **SCALE PATTERN**

330 **FLEXIBILITY**

331 **ARPEGGIOS**

332 **INTERVALS**

333 BALANCE AND INTONATION: MOVING CHORD TONES

334 BALANCE AND INTONATION: SHIFTING CHORD QUALITIES

335 EXPANDING INTERVALS: DOWNWARD IN PARALLEL OCTAVES

336 EXPANDING INTERVALS: UPWARD IN PARALLEL FIFTHS

337 CONCERT G MAJOR SCALE AND CHORALE

Chris M. Bernotas (ASCAP)

338 CHORALE

Stephen Melillo (ASCAP)

In full glory!

339 CHORALE

Andrew Boysen, Jr.

Slow and peaceful

Concert E Minor (Your F# Minor)

340 LONG TONES

341 CONCERT E NATURAL MINOR SCALE

342 CONCERT E HARMONIC AND MELODIC MINOR SCALES

harmonic minor scale   melodic minor scale

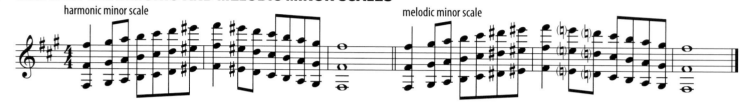

343 SCALE PATTERN

344 SCALE PATTERN

345 FLEXIBILITY

346 ARPEGGIOS

49

347 **INTERVALS**

348 **BALANCE AND INTONATION: LAYERED TUNING**

349 **BALANCE AND INTONATION: DIATONIC HARMONY**

350 **EXPANDING INTERVALS: DOWNWARD IN PARALLEL FIFTHS**

351 **EXPANDING INTERVALS: DOWNWARD IN TRIADS**

352 **CONCERT E MINOR SCALE AND CHORALE**

Chris M. Bernotas (ASCAP)

353 **CHORALE**

Michael Story (ASCAP)

Moderato

354 **CHORALE**

Chris M. Bernotas (ASCAP)

Mournfully

Concert A Major (Your B Major)

355   **CONCERT A MAJOR SCALE AND CHORDS**

356   **SCALE PATTERN**

357   **BALANCE AND INTONATION: MOVING CHORD TONES**

358   **CHORALE**

Chris M. Bernotas (ASCAP)

Concert F♯ Minor (Your G♯ Minor)

359   **CONCERT F♯ NATURAL MINOR SCALE AND CHORDS**

360   **CONCERT F♯ HARMONIC AND MELODIC MINOR SCALES**

harmonic minor scale   melodic minor scale

361   **SCALE PATTERN**

362   **BALANCE AND INTONATION: LAYERED TUNING**

363   **CHORALE**

Chris M. Bernotas (ASCAP)

Concert D Major (Your E Major)

64 **CONCERT D MAJOR SCALE AND CHORDS**

65 **SCALE PATTERN**

66 **BALANCE AND INTONATION: MOVING CHORD TONES**

67 **CHORALE**

Chris M. Bernotas (ASCAP)

Concert B Minor (Your C♯ Minor)

68 **CONCERT B NATURAL MINOR SCALE AND CHORDS**

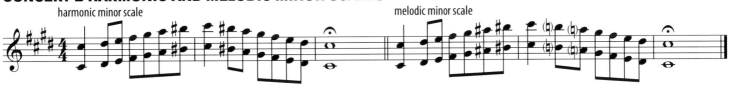

69 **CONCERT B HARMONIC AND MELODIC MINOR SCALES**

70 **SCALE PATTERN**

71 **BALANCE AND INTONATION: LAYERED TUNING**

72 **CHORALE**

Chris M. Bernotas (ASCAP)

Concert B/C♭ Major (Your D♭ Major)

373 **CONCERT B/C♭ MAJOR SCALE AND CHORDS**

374 **SCALE PATTERN**

375 **BALANCE AND INTONATION: PERFECT INTERVALS**

376 **CHORALE**

Chris M. Bernotas (ASCAP)

Concert G♯/A♭ Minor (Your B♭ Minor)

377 **CONCERT G♯/A♭ NATURAL MINOR SCALE AND CHORDS**

378 **CONCERT G♯/A♭ HARMONIC AND MELODIC MINOR SCALES**

379 **SCALE PATTERN**

380 **BALANCE AND INTONATION: MOVING CHORD TONES**

381 **CHORALE**

Chris M. Bernotas (ASCAP)

Concert E Major (Your F# Major)

382 CONCERT E MAJOR SCALE AND CHORDS

383 SCALE PATTERN

384 BALANCE AND INTONATION: LAYERED TUNING

385 CHORALE

Chris M. Bernotas (ASCAP)

Concert C# Minor (Your D# Minor)

386 CONCERT C# NATURAL MINOR SCALE AND CHORDS

387 CONCERT C# HARMONIC AND MELODIC MINOR SCALES

harmonic minor scale

melodic minor scale

388 SCALE PATTERN

389 BALANCE AND INTONATION: MOVING CHORD TONES

390 CHORALE

Chris M. Bernotas (ASCAP)

Concert F#/Gb Major (Your Ab Major)

391   **CONCERT F#/Gb MAJOR SCALE AND CHORDS**

392   **SCALE PATTERN**

393   **BALANCE AND INTONATION: PERFECT INTERVALS**

394   **CHORALE**

Chris M. Bernotas (ASCAP)

Concert Eb Minor (Your F Minor)

395   **CONCERT Eb NATURAL MINOR SCALE AND CHORDS**

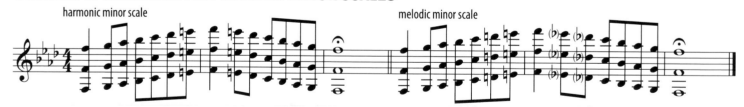

396   **CONCERT Eb HARMONIC AND MELODIC MINOR SCALES**

harmonic minor scale   melodic minor scale

397   **SCALE PATTERN**

398   **BALANCE AND INTONATION: LAYERED TUNING**

399   **CHORALE**

Chris M. Bernotas (ASCAP)

Clarinet Fingering Chart

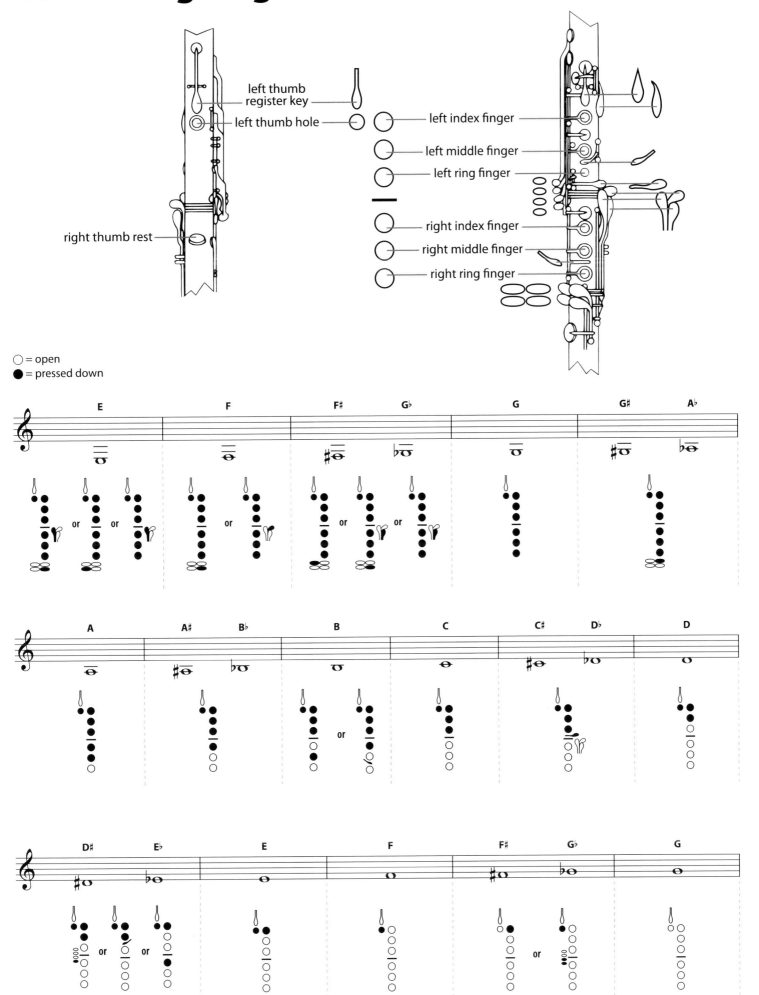

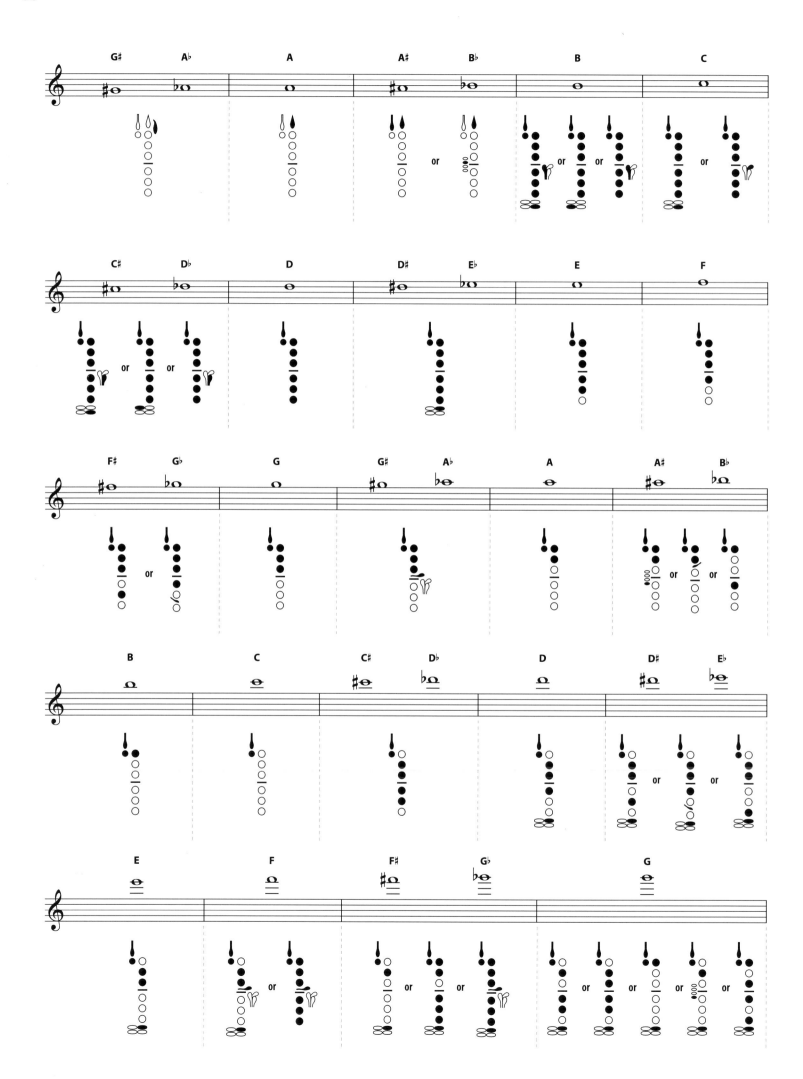